A Quiet Loss

Tom Ferguson

ISBN:9798553940584

DEDICATION

To Kimberly, Joey, Janey, John, and Violet

ACKNOWLEDGMENTS

Thanks to my wife, Cindy, and my daughters Sommer and Skye, for sharing many thoughts on their painful experiences. Thanks to Sandra Miller for reviewing the manuscript and providing beautiful insights and suggestions.

<u>PREFACE</u>

These were harrowing stories to write.   If you have experienced this loss as a parent, I pray you would see the way forward in faith. I hope you can gain insight and perhaps comfort someone you know who is grieving for those of you who have not suffered this loss.

These stories are generational. The first story is about an adult son listening to his mother.   The son and his wife suffer the loss of a child, then years later, their two daughters also suffer losses.

These stories are loosely based on real-life experience but are not intended to be a factual description of anyone's personal experience. Many of the events have been changed for dramatic effect. Some of the particular accounts are entirely fictional. The overall book then should be read as a novel.

What is real? The feelings, the emotions, the grief, the sorrow, the prayers, and the faith – those are real. The book's purpose is to give the reader a glimpse of what this pain – this quiet loss - is like for a family.

1 AN ISSUE OF BLOOD

And a woman was there who had been subject to bleeding for twelve years. She had suffered a great deal under the care of many doctors and had spent all she had, yet instead of getting better she grew worse. Mark 5:25,26 NIV

She told me this story not long before she died. It was not the first time I had heard it.

I knew something was wrong, so I ran home from school. Aunt O. met me at the door and said everything was fine, but I knew it wasn't right. Despite what she said, I ran straight to Mamma's room. Blood! It seemed to be everywhere, all over Mamma, the sheets, and the towels scattered on the floor.

She paused and sighed as she began to cry.

Then she asked me if I was supposed to be at school. I told her I had already been to school. Just then, they had finally got a doctor, but he was drunk. I was only twelve years old. I smelled it on his breath as he went past me. He said she had lost the baby and was very weak and tired as if we couldn't see that.

She waited, her eyes going back and forth furiously as if reliving it, the memory summoning the still bitter rage against what she had witnessed.

THEN, he gave her some chloroform to rest, he said. She gasped one more breath and then fell back dead. She died!

She paused to demonstrate the gasping sound for me.

All of them just standing around, worried about Uncle P. instead of my Mamma. They should have gotten her to the hospital for a blood transfusion. Someone should have done something. They could have done something.

Her eyes closed, and soon her regular breath told me she was asleep. I crept out of the hospital room to get some coffee.

A Quiet Loss

My eyes will flow unceasingly,
without relief,
until the LORD looks down
from heaven and sees.
What I see brings grief to my soul
because of all the women of my city.

Lamentations 3:49-51 (NIV)

Book One

STONE OF REMEMBRANCE

3

For Kimberly Dawn

1 A Long View

For the revelation awaits an appointed time

Habakkuk 2:3 NIV

"James," he replied. She smiled. It was the married couples first discussion of baby names.

"That's funny because I have always wanted a son named James – after my Dad, of course!" she replied.

"My grandfather was named James Thomas, and I've always wanted to name a son after him. I've always wanted to have a son," he replied thoughtfully. She smiled again and paused, thinking about how to open this next topic.

"I have to tell you something, and it may sound weird. It happened a long time ago, but I can tell you about it now that we are engaged," she began. A puzzled look came over his face.

"Go ahead, I mean, is it bad or something?" he replied.

"You remember right after we first met, when I worked at the mall, you came out one night to buy winter clothes?"

"Yes, that was in late September, right after I first came," he replied.

"I was working that night, and I saw you coming towards me. I think you noticed I was quiet for a few seconds when you first walked up."

"You know, I think I do remember that. I think you smiled though – one of the things I really liked about you when we first met was your smile! So, why the delay?"

"As soon as I saw you, a vision just came into my head. I saw us together, married, and I was holding our baby boy. I was so stunned by the vision I could not speak for a few seconds."

"So, that's why you wanted to talk about boy names tonight?"

"Yes. Because I know we are going to have a boy."

> *"What's in a name? that which we call a rose*
> *By any other name would smell as sweet."*
>
> Romeo and Juliet, Shakespeare

2 THE GOLDEN SHORE

What is it like?

Do you mean how does it feel?

Have you ever heard her voice?

No. I cannot hear her.

Tell me about her face.

I cannot. I am blinded by the light behind her.

Have you really seen her?

No, I am sure I only imagine that I see her. She is too real for me to see.

How does it make you feel?

I feel her reproach that I have not thought of her. But I am quite sure those are my guilty thoughts—a false guilt of relief.

Explain.

She is in a place of love and only love. There is no reproach except in my wounded soul.

Where is she?

She is in a real place. I am in a world of smoke and dreams.

Do you miss her?

I wish I could miss her.

Do you think she knows you?

I will know her.

You will not abandon me to the realm of the dead,
nor will you let your faithful one know decay. Acts 2:27 NIV

3 THE TIMING

Now we see through a glass – darkly, but then face to face…

1 Corinthians 13: 12 KJV

"Remember what happened last year," she reminded him. It had only been eight months since the first miscarriage.

"Still, I think we could tell our families now. My sister has already told them she is expecting," he responded.

"Yeah, you told me that. That will be their third child!" she replied wistfully. After a moment, she continued.

"I want to wait a little longer. Then we can call the family and play the 'guess what?' game," she added. He shrugged. It was up to her, after all. Everyone had been so excited last year when they had announced the first pregnancy. Their excitement made it difficult – embarrassing, really – to make that next call and tell them that was over.

"You didn't say anything. So, is it okay if we wait another week? Or maybe two?" she queried.

"You are right. Let's wait another week. Can we start talking about names now, though?" he replied, adding, "I think it is going to be a little girl!"

"But remember my vision! I am sure we will have a boy!" she exclaimed.

I was given a glass box full of broken glass

I held it up to the sun

To see the danger and the beauty of it.

4 OUT OF SOUL

The soul separates sight unseen

Who knows the time she takes her leave?

Poor boy or English queen

First the loss, then you grieve.

Who can say when night will end?

As light fades out in the western sky

Of death, the darkness doth portend!

My Redeemer will stand upon the earth

I know not when or how

Then my soul will prove its worth

Before him, I will bow.

Death overtakes us all.

Every death announces the Fall.

5 HAPPY BIRTHDAY

Teach us to number our days, that we may gain a heart of wisdom. Psalm 90:12 NIV

Tuesday:

"Where do you want to eat out for your birthday?" he asked. She had just come in from work.

"Wait, you know I had a sonogram today. Everything looks great!" she smiled.

"Well, that's encouraging! Are we having a boy or a girl?"

"Too early to tell."

Twelve days later, a Sunday:

"Ohhhh!"

"What's wrong?" he whispered. It was the middle of the Sunday morning service.

"Huge kick!" she whispered in reply. She wondered at the intensity of the jolt. Was something wrong?

Twenty days later, a Monday:

"This can't be right," she told herself. She slipped the maternity pants off and grabbed a pair of regular jeans from the back of the closet. They fit fine, zipping up all the way. Her stomach was flatter. She had not felt the baby move since the big kick twenty days ago.

Something is wrong. She decided to make the call.

"Village Obstetrics, how may I help you?"

"I'm worried something has happened to my baby."

I made a castle, drizzling the wet sand through my fingers to form fantastic tiny shapes. I watched as the waves came in to wash them all away.

6 A LONG WEEKEND

My soul is in deep anguish.
How long, LORD, how long? Psalm 6:3 NIV

Friday:

"I still can't believe it," he said, picking at his food. She did not look up.

"It is a hard time to be alone," she replied flatly.

"I told work I was going to have to take off on Monday. We have to be there at 8:00 am, right?" he asked.

"Yes. They said it would take about eight hours."

"They are sure?"

"There is no heartbeat. It's going to be a long weekend waiting for Monday.

Saturday:

She read. She talked to her Mom and sister a little when they called.

He lay in bed sort of watching Live Aid. Queen. U2. David Bowie. The acts just kept coming. It was a soundtrack to misery.

Sunday:

They went to church. No comfort there. No one noticed their obvious pain. Back to the apartment. The clock ticked off the seconds and minutes and hours until Monday.

Monday:

At the hospital at 8:00 am sharp. The tilted bed, the polite nurses, the IV medicine, everything is in order. As the induced labor commenced, she began to feel sick. More waiting, more IV bags, more nursing checks. By 5 pm, there has been almost no progress.

"The doctor had said it would take eight hours. What is happening?" she asked. The nurse grimaced.

"Probably more like twenty-four hours," she said, biting her lip.

The words hit like a thunderclap. Another whole night of misery? For what?

The evening hours dragged by. More sickness. More waiting. Messes to clean up. Sleeping two or three minutes at a time. Exhausted, he kept a weary vigil, lest he miss his child's birth.

Every tree that falls

Every salty tear

Each fallen sparrow

Each discouraged sigh.

7 Day of Darkness

What I feared has come upon me;
what I dreaded has happened to me. Job 3:25 NIV

Tuesday:

Hope against hope. They both knew there was no hope. But it was one thing to be told there is no hope and another thing to see the dead body.

It was about 8:30 am – more than the twenty-four hours of lonely misery. Time to push – just like giving birth to a live baby, explained the nurse. Here comes the little girl – not too hard; she weighed just under a pound. Perfect in form. Her color is grayish-blue because she had been in the womb so long after her demise. Her little blue eyes are open as if in shock at the light she does not see.

The nurses are polite as if the baby were alive. They all speak what sounded like well-rehearsed lines.

Look how cute she is! Oh my, she looks like her Mom! She does! Look at those blue eyes! She is so perfect!

Then comes the paperwork.

"Do you want to give her a name?"

Both the parents nod solemnly. She looks to him.

"Kimberly Dawn," the father announces.

Grandma joins them at the hospital. There is more discussion about how beautiful Kimberly Dawn is. How perfect she is!

Finally, she is alone. Her breasts are full, but her arms are empty. There is no bassinette next to her bed like the other women in the maternity ward. But she clung to the vision the Lord had given her of a baby boy.

8 A LAMENT

To be read as a lament

A voice is barely heard

Like a whisper,

An almost silent weeping,

Rachel weeps.

She weeps for her children,

She weeps because they are no more,

She weeps in dread silence,

Rachel weeps alone.

She refuses to be comforted,

Let her weep,

For her children are no more.

Let Rachel weep.

9 The Problem of Pain

"Lord, God of Israel," they cried, "why has this happened to Israel? Why should one tribe be missing from Israel today?" Judges 21:3 NIV

When a person has a limb amputated, a strange phenomenon can occur. Many amputees experience phantom pain – a pain that feels like it is coming from the limb that is no longer there. This pain is not imaginary. It may also be severe and long-lasting.

The shepherd left the ninety and nine on the hillside to see the one that was lost. It was not that the shepherd did not care for those who were saved. His focus was on what was lost.

A spirit glided past my face,
and the hair on my body stood on end. Job 4:15 NIV

10 In a Letter

…sent Hezekiah letters… because he had heard of Hezekiah's illness.

2 Kings 20:12 NIV

"How was work?" she greeted him as he opened the door.

"Kind of sad. Thought about Kim a lot," he replied, setting down his bag.

"Me too. Got a letter from Aunt Barb today. Let me read this paragraph to you," she said as she picked up the note. He sat down to listen.

I know you have been through a tragic loss. I am praying for you both that God would comfort you. In Luke 2, verse 6 speaks of the time came for the baby to be born, and she gave birth to a son.

I know the time will come, and you will have a son, and you will both rejoice at what the Lord has done.

11 Falling Through

To the roots of the mountains I sank down; the earth beneath barred me in forever. But you, Lord my God, brought my life up from the pit. Jonah 2:6 NIV

During World War Two, the Germans had Leningrad surrounded, then they waited. Inside the city, over two million people were facing slow starvation during a brutal Russian winter.

However, there was Lake Ladoga. It was to the east of Leningrad, and the far shore was outside the occupation zone. When the winter came, the lake surface froze hard enough for trucks to drive on it. These trucks could bring supplies from the other side to the starving city and take wounded and sick people out.

The lake did not freeze evenly, however. Although many trucks made it through, occasionally, a truck would hit a thin patch. If the ice broke, the vehicle would plummet to the bottom of the lake so quickly that its headlights could still be seen for a short time.

No one stopped to help. There was nothing the passersby could do anyway. Some fall through the ice – quietly. The others go on serenely, perhaps not even realizing the danger.

After the servant had lifted him up and carried him to his mother, the boy sat on her lap until noon, and then he died. 2 Kings 4:20 NIV

12 Entropy

I imagined her beauty in full flower

Grand in her maturity like a stately home

But a great storm brought a mighty wind

And that wind toppled a tree

There it fell on the house in my vision.

The splintered wood and brick gradually collapse

A heap of broken pieces.

I will engrave her name on one stone

And keep it as a token of my dream.

13 On the Edge

My bones suffer mortal agony as my foes taunt me, saying to me all day long,
"Where is your God?"
Psalms 42:6 NIV

"But when can we go home?" the new Mom asked, wanting to hear "today" one more time. She finally had the baby boy that she had dreamed about – the one from the vision!

"Today for sure. We just need to check a few more things and get the paperwork completed. Then, after the doctor approves it, you will be on your way! Now, I'm going to take the baby down to the nursery so you can just get some rest," the nurse explained as she reached out to take the baby. The new Mom grudgingly released the infant and smiled at him as he was taken. After the nurse left, she did fall asleep for a few minutes.

She awoke with a start. There were two doctors she had never seen before, along with the nurse.

"We have news for you," the older doctor began.

"Good news? Or bad?" she replied.

"It's bad news," he said, pausing briefly.

"Your child stopped breathing."

But as for me, my feet had almost slipped; I had nearly lost my foothold.
Psalm 73:2 NIV

14 Hailstorm

My eyes grow weak with sorrow

Psalm 6:7 NIV

The new father was at home, preparing to go to the hospital. Today would be the day! Mom and the new baby were coming home!

Then came the call. Unexpected. Perplexing. Then heart-rending.

"It's bad… stopped breathing…he turned black… NICU…kidney damage…brain damage…blindness…will he live…not sure…when can you come…we need to tell family."

Another trip to the hospital to face death. More disappointment. A blizzard of questions. Empty arms. Again.

Therefore groan, son of man! Groan before them with broken heart and bitter grief.
Ezekiel 21:6 NIV

15 Desperate Prayer

Hear my cry for mercy as I call to you for help

Psalm 28:2 NIV

He made it through the first twenty-four hours. He looks big next to all those preemies! He looks healthy! Dare we hope?

During the day, another seizure. Then another. Something is wrong. Terribly wrong. Doctor seen pointing and shaking his head. Was he pointing at our baby? I don't know.

Prayer. Face down. Stretched out.

Dear Lord, heal our son, our only son. Have mercy on him. And on us.

16 Christmas Miracle

For unto us, a child is born, and unto us, a son is given.

Isaiah 9:6 NIV

Day 11: "You can take him home after you, and your husband have both completed infant CPR training. You must remember – either the baby is on a heart monitor, or you are watching him – at all times! His heart could stop again at any time."

Day 28: "Guess what? I had him near the vanity so I could fix my hair and still see him in the mirror. He followed me with his eyes! He is not blind!"

Day 180: "We disconnect the heart monitor tonight. Can we sleep? Or will we be worried and lie awake all night?"

You can stay awake, or you can trust in Me.

Day 330: The pediatric neurologist smiled. This boy is fine. In fact, he is advanced! You need not bring him back to me again.

Heal me, LORD, and I will be healed; save me and I will be saved, for you are the one I praise. Jeremiah 17:14 NIV

17 A Letter Unsent

Your nickname: Kim

What you called me: I never got to hear your voice

Dear Kimberly Dawn,

I remember you. I do not know how to get this letter to you, so I will send it to your brother and sisters. I think about you from time to time. Sometimes years go by and then sometimes I think about you a lot. I have thought about you a lot more since baby Violet joined you in heaven. I often picture the two of you together. You are a little taller than Violet in my dreams. You are both dressed in white and have long hair. Violet's hair is white blonde, and yours is a beautiful brown. I cannot see your face or hear you say anything – there are no messages from that side. I just know you are my daughter.

First memories:

I remember holding you for the only time. You were so tiny! So many tears over your loss. Your face reminds me now of your little sister. I think you would have enjoyed playing with your brother and sisters.   They would have loved to have a big sister on earth.

Your grandmother June got to hold you too. She said you were beautiful – which we already knew! It was a precious day on that Tuesday in July 1985. The only day we saw you and held you. You were so perfect. There was nothing wrong with you. For some reason, your little heart had stopped. When we found out you were dead, your Mom and I were heartbroken.

The unanswerable questions – what happened? Why did we lose you? How would things be different if you had grown up here on earth? I do not know the answers. I know I love you, and I always will. One day we will all see you and see your beautiful smile, and there will be no more tears. One day I will hold you again and never say farewell.

Your Dad

18 STONE OF REMEMBRANCE

He buried him… in the valley…, but to this day no one knows where his grave is.

Deuteronomy 34:6 NIV

What did we do with the body? We were strangers in a strange land. No grave plot, no savings to draw on. Her body was donated to science. There was no funeral, no burial, no mourners but us two.

Thirty-three years later, we began to assemble a Memory Garden. Expressing our loss through the building of a special place, we remember the lives of our missing babies. A concrete angel we call Grace looks over the garden. Our youngest daughter lettered a simple marker and we placed it in the garden under the angel's benevolent gaze.

Kimberly Dawn

July 16, 1985

Precious daughter

He will wipe every tear from their eyes. Revelation 21:4 NIV

Book Two
Dreams After the Storm

Dedication

To Violet June, precious and beautiful flower

1 PREDICTION

And God remembered her, and God hearkened to her, and opened her womb

Genesis 30:22 KJV

Kaye is getting Clarise into the car seat after church, hoping to leave soon since she is hungry. Levi is still talking to people as usual. Kaye gets in the passenger side, starts the car, and turns the air conditioner on full blast. At last, Levi comes to the vehicle.

"Where do you want to eat lunch?" she asks.

"Oh, we are going with Essie and Leon to McAlester's. Okay?"

"Sure. Guess what Cathy told me?" Kaye looked over at Levi for a reaction. There was no response.

"I said, GUESS what Cathy told me!"

"Oh, sorry, I was trying to pull out of the parking lot. I don't know. What did she say?"

"She said I'm going to have a little girl!" Kay said with excitement.

"Well, that's great, but how does she know? Do you know something I don't?" Kaye shook her head.

"No, I'm not pregnant yet. But we have been praying. Remember we went forward for prayer, and Cathy and Bob prayed for us?"

"Daddy, I'm going to have a baby sister!" Clarise chimed in from the back seat. Levi glanced at her smiling face in the rearview mirror.

"Someday, baby. Someday you will have a little sister. You will be the best big sister ever!"

"Yessssss!"

"I had a dream last night."

"What was it?"

"I was looking for treasure in a field. After I had searched for a while, I noticed there were sheep following me. Soon sheep were streaming towards me from everywhere. It became more and more difficult to search."

"What happened?"

"Finally, I could not move at all. The sheep were jammed all around me, not hurting me; I simply could not move. I knew the treasure was close by, but I could not move."

"Is that the nature of sheep?"

"I do not know. I think it may be the nature of dreams."

2 KNOWING

For you created my inmost being.
You knit me together in my mother's womb.

"I want to know. No, I don't want to know. What if it's no? No, it will be yes. I want to know. Okay, I'm going to look. No, I'll wait till he gets home. If I find out now, I won't be able not to tell Clarise. Or she will figure it out! She's so smart! But I want to know. Okay, I'm going to look. Here goes!"

She looked and smiled and began to cry. She peeked out of the bathroom to see if Clarise was still asleep. Kaye tiptoed over and squeezed in next to the snoozing two-year-old. Carefully she slid the tiny head up onto her lap and gently stroked the beautiful brown hair.

"I'm home! What's this? Both my beautiful girls asleep!"

Kaye stirred herself to get off the couch and went to hug Levi.

"Guess what," she whispered into his ear.

He pushed her back while still embracing her.

"What? Guess what?"

"Just guess," she said invitingly. Levi looked at the gleam of joy in her eyes. That could only mean one thing.

"Really?" he asked.

She nodded, and they embraced again and kissed.

"Does Clarise know?" It was his turn to whisper in her ear.

"Umm… mmm."

"What about Essie? Did you tell her? Because if you did, then she told Leon, which means my brother found out before me."

"No, no, no, you are the first!" Kaye smiled.

"We prayed so long. I was beginning to wonder." Levi said wistfully.

"I know. But I think Clarise knew. Just last week, remember? She put her hand on my tummy and said, "Mommy's gonna have a baby girl!"".

Levi nodded.

"Hi Daddy," Clarise called out from the couch, sitting up. The couple looked at each other and nodded.

"Guess what, baby? Big news!" Levi said.

Clarise looked at Mommy. She had a big smile.

"Mommy gonna have a baby sister for me!" she said, her bright eyes shining with joy.

"How did you know, bunny rabbit!" Kaye said excitedly.

"I just did. I already knew it was time," Clarise said quite decisively for a two-year-old. It was time for a family hug. Levi pulled back and exhaled.

"Well, who are we going to tell next? Essie and Leon? My parents? Your parents?"

"Let's call our sister and brother. Then you can tell your parents, and I'll tell mine." Kaye suggested, still holding Clarise.

"Boy or girl? What do you think?" he asked.

"GIRL!" Clarise interjected.

"I'll be happy with either. But I bet your Dad wants a boy this time."

"NO BOYS! BABY SISTER FOR ME!" Clarise said insistently.

Levi shrugged.

"Let's eat first, and we can talk about it. Then we will start making our calls."

"I tell Aunt Essie! I tell Aunt Essie!"

"Okay, little bunny, you can tell her. But first, wash hands so we can eat."

"It will be my first food with a baby sister!"

"I had a dream."
"What was it?"
"She is about twenty. She says, don't worry about her; she's okay."
"I want to have a dream."

I created you, my child, my precious Violet.
You have seen my substance as yet being unperfect.
Child, you are not hidden from me, even though you are in secret.
Lead me in the way everlasting.

3 ANNOUNCEMENT

The lot is cast into the lap; but the whole disposing thereof is of the Lord.

Proverbs 16:33 KJV

"I just hope everyone can be there," Kaye said as she wrote another little note. She carefully unscrewed the plastic egg, placed the message inside, and put the egg back together.

"Do you think this is the right time to tell everyone?" Levi asked. Kaye was already opening another egg.

"I feel pretty good about it by now."

"Yeah, but it was just last Thanksgiving that Essie had that miscarriage." Kaye's face darkened.

"I know. I felt bad for them. But I feel fine with this one. There, that should be enough eggs. I hope Mom and Dad can get back from the cabin in time. Your Mom will be with us, and everyone else is coming too."

"Where are we eating again?" Levi inquired. Kaye shook her head.

"I already told you – SPRING CREEK BARBEQUE," she said as she began putting the eggs into a basket.

"Oh, that's right.

Everyone did make it to Spring Creek, and Kaye, Levi, and Clarise enjoyed passing out the eggs.

"Now open your eggs! Special message inside!" Kaye said brightly.

Mom was the first one to get one open.

"Hey, you are having another baby!" she exclaimed. Lots of hugs and handshakes and laughter ensued, and everyone began guessing boy or girl.

""Are you going with me on Monday?" Kaye asked.

"Sure. Are we going to find out then?"

"Yes, I hope so. She said they can usually tell by then. I think it's a boy."

"But you really want another girl, don't you?" Levi asked. Kaye was quiet for a long time.

"Yes. But I have been praying about it, and God has softened my heart. I am ready to have a boy now," she said thoughtfully.

"That's good. I mean, we should be thankful to the Lord for the baby, whether boy or girl," Levi added.

"True. If it is a girl, though, what will we name her?" Kaye said slyly.

"Isabella," he responded. Kaye shrugged.

<break>

"Let's see. We should have the image up shortly – there it is! Okay, well, this one is not too hard. It's a girl!" the technician said confidently. Kaye and Levi looked at each other.

"Isabella," Levi said with a firm nod.

"My Mom had a dream while we were there."
"What was it?"
"She saw a baby girl. She was sick. Something was wrong with her face."
"Does she think it was our baby?"
"I don't know."

4 REVEAL

But there is a God in heaven that revealeth secrets…

Daniel 2:28 KJV

"I think we should just write the word 'girl' on the wall and cover it up," Kaye said.

"Sounds good. Then, we pull the cover off after everyone has guessed?" Levi responded.

"Right. Everyone is making it so complicated these days. Let's keep it simple."

"Are we going to reveal the name too?"

"Well, let's not do that yet. I want to talk about it with you."

"Sure. Now, what are the guesses? Has anyone said?"

"I put in on FB. Mom says, 'boy,' Dad says 'girl,' Essie says 'boy.' Still waiting for a few more to respond."

I dreamed I was sent on a secret mission. I was assigned to follow someone and listen to his conversation, but I was not told why. I followed him to the airport to fly to another country. I knew I had to follow, even though I did not want to go. Then, they would not let me through the gate, and I saw the plane fly away without me.

5 NAMES

And thou shalt take two onyx stones, and engrave on them the names of the children of Israel…

Exodus 28:9 KJV

"But what does it mean?" she asked.

"It is the Spanish form of Elizabeth. It means 'devoted to God' according to what I read," he replied. Kaye nodded her head thoughtfully.

"So, you get to pick the middle name then," Levi said with a laugh.

"I like the name 'Elise,'" she replied. Levi took out his phone.

"Google, background on the name Elise."

"Elise is a name of French origin equivalent to the name Elizabeth," the phone replied in its best helpful voice. Kaye and Levi laughed together.

"So, her name will be 'Elizabeth Elizabeth'!" he said.

"Agreed!" Kay said with a big smile, "It's perfect."

"She is doubly devoted to God!"

No, I didn't talk to her. I just sensed she was looking at me, and I knew that she loved me. I could not see her face. THAT was the dream.

6 THIEF

The thief comes only to steal and kill and destroy…

John 10:10 NIV

"There's one!" Romeo cried out, suddenly slowing to a crawl. Jorge jumped out and ran to the porch as Romeo turned the car around.

"It's a big one!" Jorge said, tossing it in the back seat, "no room for this in the trunk."

"Hey, you! I'm calling the cops!"

"Quick, let's go!"

The tires squealed as Romeo launched the car out of the tight cul-de-sac. He turned right on Corporate Drive and headed towards I-35E.

"Do you think she got our license number?" asked Jorge.

"I don't know. Play it cool. Slit that box open quick-like and see what we got."

Jorge took out his knife and leaned back over the seat to open the package.

"It looks like an infant seat. You know, for a car – DUDE! COPS!"

<break>

Levi woke with a start. He hated that falling dream. Kaye was lying on her side, looking at him.

"Check your phone. See if you heard from the police," she said.

"Good morning to you too! Are you taking me to work?"

"Well, first, check your phone."

He grabbed the iPhone off the nightstand.

"Amazon says the driver confirms the box was delivered. Police say yes, a neighbor reported a porch pirate – says they saw them take the box. The police say they did track down the car, but there was only one person in it and no box visible."

"Well, great. They probably threw it in a dumpster and played innocent. Now when we drive past the landfill, we can say hi to Violet's car seat."

"Amazon said they will replace it when we file this police report."

"But Levi – it's almost Christmas, and Violet is due any minute! How are we going to bring her home from the hospital without a proper infant seat?"

"I don't know. Maybe we borrow one. Are you taking me to work?"

"No, Clarise is still asleep. We will just stay home today. Hey, did you have another dream?"

"Yes, I did," said Levi as he buttoned his work shirt.

"Was it about Violet?" she asked very quietly.

"No, I think it was about falling. I have to go. Gonna be late."

<email ding>

"Was that from Amazon? Check! Quick!"

Levi paused and pulled his phone back out. He read the email and gradually frowned.

"What's wrong?" Kaye demanded.

"They don't have any more of those," he said glumly.

"WHAT! But it was perfect! And we need it NOW!"

"They have this one," he said, showing her the phone.

"I don't WANT that one! I don't WANT a replacement!"

"What difference does it make? I'm going to order it. It'll be here on Saturday.

Kaye collapsed at the kitchen table. She put her head on her arms and began to sob.

"I DON'T WANT THAT ONE! I WANT THE ONE I ORDERED! It's my fault. I should have been home sooner."

"Look, there's nothing we can do about it. Gotta go for sure now." She did not even hear the door shut.

I dreamed of her again. She never talks, and I can never see her face clearly because of the blazing light behind her. I feel sad that for a time, I have forgotten about her. She is still mine even though she is not here with me.

7 SOFTER

For God maketh my heart soft and the Almighty troubleth me
Job 23:16 KJV

"What's wrong?" Levi asked. It is dinner time, and Kaye is very quietly picking at her food. She shrugged.

"I really want another girl," she began.

"Oh, and you know I wish we had a boy, right?" Levi put down his fork.

"Right. And I've thought about it a lot," she replied. Levi smiled.

"And what have you decided?" he asked.

"I will love our baby, whether it is a boy or girl," she announced firmly.

"And what changed?"

"Well, I have prayed about this, and God has softened my heart. I know now that I can love a girl because we already have Clarise. I will love the next one too – boy or girl."

The south wind blew softly, and they supposed they had obtained their purpose. So, they sailed close to the shore. Not long afterwards, a tempestuous wind arose. And we, being exceedingly tossed by the wind, lightened the ship with our own hands. Neither sun nor stars in many days appeared. Acts 27:13-15 KJV, paraphrased by the author

8 FINALLY

Rejoice, thou barren that bearest not; break forth and cry, thou that travailest not.
Galatians 4:27, KJV

"What are we doing for New Year's Eve? Have you talked to Essie today?" Levi asked.

"Maybe we will be at the midwife's having a baby," Kaye responded with a smile, patting her stomach.

"What? Are you in labor?" he inquired.

"I am having a few pains. I mean, she is six days overdue. Maybe this is it!" she spoke softly.

"So, we should get ready to go? Did you call the midwife?"

"Not just yet. Let me lie down on the couch for a few minutes and see if it progresses."

In the dream, I saw in my hands the tools of my trade. Before me, on a white table, were the materials needed to complete the task. In my mind, however, I found no knowledge to proceed. I laid the tools on the table. I bowed my head and wept in great sorrow. When I finally lifted my head, I saw that my tears had dissolved the table and all that was on it.

9 MOVE

The wind bloweth where it listeth, and thou hearest the sound thereof, but canst not tell whence it cometh, and whither it goeth John 3:8 KJV

"Happy New Year!" Dad greeted the group as he and Mom took their place at the table.

"Yes, yes, here we are at Spring Creek again," Kaye said brightly. Her face shone with the expectation of new life. Yesterday, there was some false labor, but it could not be much longer now.

The conversation drifts here and there, plans and thoughts, New Year's resolutions, and many trivial things. But Kaye is thinking only of holding Violet in her arms.

"Soon," she says to herself.

I dreamed that a plague of darkness came over the land — a night that could be felt. I could not see or be seen. There was nothing to do but wait for it to end. My cries for help vanished into the foreboding night.

10 LAST

She drew her feet up and breathed her last and was gathered to her home.
Genesis 49:33 KJV paraphrased by the author

For who knows a person's thoughts but their own spirit within them?
1 Corinthians 2:11 KJV paraphrased by the author

Eleven-thirty a.m. at the kitchen table – the one she had sat so many times growing up. Her thoughts are cloudy with a storm on the horizon.

A jolt goes through her. She kicked! Maybe she is fine, after all?

There is no further movement. Nor will there be. The storm breaks forth, and the torrents of rain begin to pour down.

In my dream, I saw the storm coming. I was in a shelter with my family, and my father had the door slightly ajar to see outside. He took my hand and lifted me so I could see out as well. A great thunderclap exploded above us, and the lightning lit up the field as at noonday. I saw a branch fall out of the nearest tree, and with it fell a tiny sparrow. The bird lay there near the branch, and I wanted to rescue him, but my father constrained me. I could not hold back my tears. My father took me and held me in his arms.

11 WHIRLWIND

His way is in the whirlwind and the storm
Nahum 1:3 NIV

They said they can't find it. She can't find it. They didn't find it. No! No! No! Dear Lord, no! What about this white dress? It's for her!

There must be something wrong. Maybe something is wrong. This can't be right. Try again. TRY AGAIN! NO!

Mommy! Daddy! Help me! Someone help me! Oh, please, someone, help me! Mommy! Daddy! MOMMY! DADDY!

Is something wrong? Deafening silence. We are lost. Where is it? Where do we go? I don't see the way. It's too dark! Call someone. Call everyone. CALL EVERYONE! HELP! Are you sure it's not a mistake? Tears. It's too cold. We can't stop here — this is not the place. Why did you spill that?

O Lord, please help! It can't be. This can't be. O Lord, loosen my lips! Help me to pray! Save! Please save!

Silent desperation.

If I had anything to give, I would give it for you. Please. Anything. Kimberly. Like with Kimberly. Why did you forget me? She can't speak.

How can you be hungry? Terrifying stillness. I can hear my heartbeat. Why can I hear it? What did they say? I didn't hear them — what did they say?

I can't find a door. It's already open. I can't close it now. It must be closed. Something is terribly wrong. How do I wake up? I've got to wake up. How long?

I can't believe what happened. I want to wake up. I need to sleep.

I can't tell you why. I don't know why. Why? I don't know what to say. Say something — say anything. Tell me something? What did they say? Anything?

Silence.

Sometimes the answer to prayer is silence. It may be a loud silence full of meaning for the one who has ears to hear. I heard that silence at the end of this prayer — so much prayer. Prayers for a miracle of restoration, for life, for a spark of hope, for a resurrection, for a healing. The answer was silence.

The silence was full of love and comfort. There was the knowledge imparted to me that I had been heard but that she was home now and was not coming back. His ways are higher.

We can ask. We must ask. We must then receive His answer.

12 SEPARATION

Precious in the sight of the Lord

"Did I doze off?" Kaye said sleepily. The half-lit room was quiet except for the whirring and beeping of modern medicine.

"Yes. For a few minutes." Levi responded sleepily.

"What time is it?" she asked. He looked at his phone.

"About 2 am."

"Do you think Clarise is okay with my parents? She has never been away from us overnight."

Levi shrugged and let the question fall. He was too tired to think. The door opened, and a nurse peeked in before entering. She smiled at Kaye and looked over the readings.

"Everything looks good. The doctor will come in and check you soon. Do you feel okay?"

"Yes," Kaye said, smiling weakly. The door opened, and the doctor strode in confidently. He nodded at the nurse, and she prepared Kaye to be examined. He was quick and efficient.

"Probably about two more hours. I'll come back at about 4 am. Let the nurse know if you have any questions." He turned and walked briskly out of the room.

"Do you need anything?" the nurse asked. Kaye shook her head no. The nurse turned and left quietly.

"Push!" the nurse implored her. Kaye was so tired. She had been through this with Clarise, but this time it was different. Catastrophically different. She gave it her best effort.

"Okay, there she is," the doctor said as he glided the baby out. Levi held Kaye's hand.

"You are done. She's here," he said, squeezing her hand gently.

"After nine months and then labor, and now I have to bury her," Kaye replied, a tear in her eye.

The medical professionals continued with their tasks.

"Time of birth 4:16 am."

"Weight: 7 pounds and 4 ounces."

"Length: 20.5 inches."

"Confirmed: No heartbeat." There was a long pause.

"Can we hold her?" asked Kaye.

"Let me get her cleaned up for you first. Then you can hold her as long as you want," the nurse replied. Kaye turned to Levi.

"Message Essie and let her know so she can tell everyone." He nodded and went back to the chair to get his phone.

<FB Msg: Violet June is here 4:16 am. No heartbeat. Pls let everyone know>.

Storms are a cleansing separation
Anything loose is washed away
The weak is easy work for the wind
Even the strong struggles in the violent test
Have you run with the foot soldiers and felt weary?
How then will you contend with horses?
If you cannot stand firm, you will not stand at all.
After you have done everything then, stand.

Tiny lamb precious lamb
Born without breath
Perfect in form
Fleeting life and then death.

13 STAY

Before tears can be dried, they must be shed.

"If we can just get her in the car." Grandpa struggled to get the crying, squirming two-year-old into the child seat.

"I just got a message from Kaye. Now they don't want us to tell her. They are going to tell her," Grandma replied.

"Just as well. It will be a moment for their family. Oh! It is so cold out here. Are we even going to remember how to get there?"

"Well, it is the same place as last night. Just a minute – I need to run back and get her 'Big Sister' shirt. They want her to wear that when she sees the baby."

<break>

"We are going to set up the lighting here in this corner." The woman spoke with a quiet tenderness while her husband opened the camera case and flipped through the lens selections. Their movements spoke to the solemnity of the occasion.

"Why don't we start with Mom and Dad, both looking at the baby?" she suggested.

Kaye propped herself up and received the tiny bundle from Levi. She positioned the baby so she and her husband could both see the little face. The room is silent except for the occasional click of the camera. The two couples shift from position to position, now just the Mom holding the baby, then the Dad, then the baby in the crib. The grandparents and Clarise arrive during the session. Clarise is kept back until Grandma can get her ready.

When Clarise is finally allowed to enter the room, she has on her "Big Sister" shirt. Mom and Dad greet her with the best smiles they can muster.

"It's your baby sister!" Kaye exclaims softly, "would you like to hold her?"

"Sure!"

Levi lifts Clarise up on to the hospital bed and helps Kaye slide the baby over into her arms, staying with her to keep her steady.

"She's your baby sister!" Grandma says in the way of encouragement.

"HI BABY SISTER!" Clarise says a little bit louder than anyone else has spoken. She turned to Kaye.

"Mommy, she needs to wake up!"

What is the worst part? The silence.

I expected her voice; her cry, her cooing laugh

I wanted to hear her

I wanted to comfort her when she cried

Instead, the stillness of the graveyard

And the cold silence of death.

14 REMEMBERING

Take twelve stones to mark where your feet stood firm in the midst of the flood

Joshua 4:3 KJV, paraphrased by author

"Can you believe this?" Kaye asked, not expecting an answer. Levi was focused on navigating the traffic back to their home, which was perfectly prepared to receive their newborn daughter.

He shook his head.

"It is hard to believe. All the waiting – now it is for nothing."

"I know. But we must never forget her. No matter how many children we have, no one will replace her. She is Violet June, and she is part of our family, and the next one will be their person, not a replacement for her." Kaye said insistently.

"I agree. We need to remember her for herself," Levi responded.

"Well, I'm going to start a baby book for her just like we planned. And I'm going to work on a list of things I want for remembrance," Kaye replied, again a little misty-eyed at the thought of the lost child.

<text message notification>.

Levi glances at his phone.

"It's a text from Mom. Read it out loud," he said, handing Kaye the phone.

"It is a Bible verse – Psalm 34:18 The LORD *is* near unto those that are of a broken heart".

"That's us," Levi replied after a pause. Kaye looked off down the road and nodded.

"I want the pain to go away, but I will never forget Violet June."

Tokens of remembrance:

1) *Her handprints and footprints*
2) *A jar of dirt from her grave*
3) *Outfit she wore*
4) *Her blanket from the hospital*
5) *Her first Christmas ornament*
6) *Her hair clippings*
7) *Her mouse stuffy toy*
8) *Her funeral flower arrangement*
9) *Her bear stuffy toy*
10) *Her clothes that she never wore*
11) *Her diaper bag*
12) *Her angel from the family*

One glad morning

I'll see you

And I'll touch you

And at last

I will see your smile.

Until then

I will think of you

And dream of you

And remember you

Will I forget you?

No, I will never, ever forget you

My precious flower.

15 FAREWELL

…comfort one another with these words.

1 Thessalonians 4:18 KJV

Jesus wept. John 11:35 KJV

On a beautiful and bright day, a crisp and cloudless sky rests over Golden Cemetery. A black Suburban serves as the hearse. The back door opens, and the tiny white coffin is carried to the graveside by two men. A tent has been set up, and twelve chairs for the family are under it. There are thirty others gathered, standing interspersed with the surrounding gravestones.

"Family and friends, we are gathered here to remember Violet June. The family greatly appreciates your support during this difficult time."

"I knew Violet! She liked to shop! She liked to go get Andy's Custard!"

"God can explain. We cannot understand. The limitation is on our part, not his. We must rely on his steadfast love."

"This is a hard thing. Life is full of hard things, but the Lord is with us."

"We appreciate you being here and your love for our family."

A man picks up a guitar, and a young girl begins to sing a song. Her voice cracks, and the duo must start over. After two more futile attempts, the song about Violet is cut short.

The mourners gather into small groups. There are hugs, smiles through tears, and a deep sense of emptiness and longing. The sun is shining, but it brings no warmth.

Now the silver cord is broken,

And the pitcher is shattered at the well.

The sun has risen with scorching heat

The blossom of the beautiful flower withers

And falls to the ground,

Its beauty is now destroyed.

From Ecclesiastes 12 and James 1, KJV, paraphrased by the author

16 DREAMS

In the last days, many shall have visions, and many shall dream dreams.

From Joel 2, KJV, paraphrased by the author

I dreamed I was playing with my baby sister. We had on matching Elsa dresses, and we played in a field of flowers!

I dreamed I was on the shore of the sea, and there was a small boat there. I was curious about the ship and decided to get into it. As soon as I did, a huge wave came and took me out to sea, and soon I was ashore on a strange island. The people there took the boat away and gave me a jar of aromatic oil with a lid that did not fit. Everywhere I went, I could smell the fragrance of the oil.

In a brightly lit room, I saw her, facing away from me and talking to someone. I could not hear her voice. I asked someone, "Is that her?" "Yes, it's her."

I heard the dream. What I saw was real. I saw the other children running across the grass near the lake. They were playing chase, and the air was filled with their laughter. Then their laughter echoed off the lake and the sky, and like a dream, I heard a tiny glimpse of what eternal joy must sound like.

I dreamed we were at the mall, and Mom was holding her. The baby was wearing a fluffy pink coat, and Clarise walked with us, holding my hand.

In a rocky sunlit field, I stood, my arms raised, and my fists clenched against the sky. I see my right hand open and in it is a beautiful white stone. My left hand opens, and I see an acorn. I drop the acorn to the ground and put the stone in my pocket before turning and walking away.

17 PROMISE

O death, where is your sting?

1 Corinthians 15:55,KJV

The family files onto the platform at the Pastor's invitation. Levi is leading Clarise up the steps while Kaye holds Jacob in her arms. The grandparents are there and the aunts and uncles and cousins and even two great-aunts.

It is time now to celebrate Jacob. Violet is not forgotten, nor will she be. But a time of celebration is here.

"Will you, Levi and Kaye, bring up this child Jacob in the training and admonition of the Lord?"

"We will," they say in unison.

"To the rest of the family and the church body. Will you lift young Jacob in prayer? Will you support this family in their efforts? If you will, say AMEN!".

"AMEN!" all say, the sound echoing through the sanctuary.

"I would like to say a word. We are here on a day of joy and a day of celebration. There was a time to mourn and a time to weep. But today is a day of joy and celebration. Praise the Lord for his goodness, his faithfulness, and his steadfast love."

"I had a dream."
"Tell me about it."
"I could see her but not really make out her face. I didn't hear a voice, but I know said she loves me".

Blessed are they that mourn, for they shall be comforted.
Matthew 5:4, KJV

18 HEALING

But unto you that fear my name shall the Sun of righteousness arise with healing in his wings; and ye shall go forth… Malachi 4:2, KJV, paraphrased by author

I like to run, and I also like to play basketball. One day I was playing basketball, and I sprained my ankle. Jumping to get a rebound, my right foot came down on the opponent's foot. I fell but then got back up and played a little more, thinking it was fine. But it was not. By the time I got home, I could no longer walk on it. I could not put any weight on it at all. It hurt so badly that I could not sleep. The next morning, the ankle was very swollen and discolored. I went to the hospital for x-rays, but there was no broken bone, just a bad sprain. Walk on crutches to keep the weight off; prop it up when you get a chance, walk gingerly while it heals a little. After a while, it will get better. That was my prognosis.

After I got home, I put my crutches aside to open the door then, being new to the crutches, forgot about them and tried to step through the door. As soon as I put my right foot on the floor, my right leg gave way, and fell face down on the floor. That leg simply could not support any weight due to the injury to the ankle. I could forget that I was injured, but that did not heal the wound. I could not run for a while, even walking without crutches was out of the question.

If someone wanted to go for a walk with me, they must understand that I am injured and go at my speed. I simply cannot keep up an average pace. I am glad to say what happened to my ankle, but I do not want to dwell on it. There is no use pretending it is normal; it is not normal and healthy; the ankle is injured and needs special care.

After a week or so, I can put a little weight on the foot and begin to carefully limp around inside the house where there are things to grab for support. Gradually the ankle gets better, and I don't worry about holding on and can began to walk outside, slowly and carefully.

All my wishing and hoping for this process to go faster are in vain. The tendons, the ligaments, and other soft tissue take time to heal. They are healing every day, but to regain all the strength will take some time.

The swelling diminishes, then disappears, and the body clears the discoloration. The ankle now looks normal from the outside. But still, it is healing. It is still achy when I wake up. If I overuse it, it reminds me quite sharply that it is not ready for full-time work.

At last, I can try to run again. Carefully I proceed, only for short distances, and only with the ankle wrapped in a support bandage for protection. I am running again – but not at regular speed and not for the distances I was accustomed to.

Now, much time has gone by, and I can walk, run, and even play basketball again. Still, sometimes I step off a curb awkwardly, and my right leg gives way with a sharp stab of pain, another reminder that the healing process is not quite complete. Everything may be back in place, but there is still a strengthening needed. That will take time and work.

I will never forget her. The pain of losing her was immense. We lost her, both of us. Our whole family lost her – grandparents, aunts, and uncles, cousins – all of us lost her. It hurt.

My faith is strong. Our faith is strong. Like the house built on the rock, we withstood the storm when it crashed against us. Our physical bodies were not damaged, nor were our minds. We can still think, reason, read, and write! However, something within me is injured. There is no use pretending otherwise. I and we cannot merely function like the day before yesterday. It will take time to heal. Some people will treat this reality awkwardly. We understand – it is awkward for you. We may look fine, but we are not fine. We want to talk about our child, maybe you don't, but we will not pretend she does not exist. We can also not pretend the pain of losing her does not exist. We cannot make the pain go away by wishing it would go away. It will take time and work.

I waited patiently for the Lord,
He turned to me, and heard my cry.
He brought me up also out of a horrible pit,
out of the miry clay.
He set my feet on a rock,
and gave me a firm place to stand.
He has put a new song in my mouth, even praise to our God.

Psalm 40, KJV, paraphrased by the author

19 MARKER

Then he took a stone and set it, and called its name Ebenezer, saying, "The Lord has helped us until now." 1 Samuel 7:12, KJV, paraphrased by the author

"Daddy, are we almost there?" Clarise asked.

"Yes, baby. Just up here," he replied, pointing toward the cemetery entrance. Levi steered the van up the narrow private lane toward the back fence and parked under the shade of a tree. He helped Clarise unbuckle and get out while Kaye lifted Jacob out of his infant seat.

"Is that the seat we got from Amazon at that time?" Levi asked. Kaye nodded without saying anything. The family made its way toward the small black marker. It was between the northern fence and many other family stones next to the grandparents' plot.

"Is this where Violet really is?" Clarise asked, tugging on Levi's arm.

"No, this is a place to remember her," he spoke softly.

"She is in heaven. We come here to remember her because her body is buried here," Kaye added helpfully.

"Oh," Clarise replied.

Kaye sets Jacob in front of her, and Levi hold Clarise next to him. He takes out his phone and snaps a picture of the marker. Everyone's feet are in the picture. It is the only family portrait.

Violet June

January 3, 2018

A moment in our arms, forever in our hearts.

We have borne the image of those made of dust; let us also bear the image of the heavenly. He will change the body of our humiliation to be conformed to the body of his glory, according to the working by which he is able even to subject all things to himself.

1 Corinthians 15:53, KJV, paraphrased by the author

20 FUTURE

At that time, Jesus answered and said, I thank thee, O Father, Lord of heaven and earth, because thou hast hid these things from the wise and prudent, and hast revealed them unto babes. Matthew 11:25 KJV

I picture her as a tiny baby because the only time I held her she was a tiny baby. That is not what she is now. Paul instructs us in 1 Corinthians 15 about the resurrection body. A seed is planted, but it bears no resemblance to the mature specimen. An acorn becomes a mighty oak, a tiny grain of mustard seed becomes a plant that is a home for the birds, and a zygote becomes a human being. Who knows what we shall be? Who knows what form those take who are asleep in Christ?

Why did this bad thing happen to me? This is an instance of the question 'Why do bad things happen to good people'? This question can be asked sincerely, but from a Christian perspective, it is based on the mistaken assumption that there are good people. There is none good but God. All have sinned and fallen short of his glory. We live in a fallen creation – a creation that Paul says groans in pain even until now. This world is in rebellion against its Creator, the LORD God Almighty. Why should anything good at all happen in this world?

Yet good things do happen. In his mercy, God sends the rain on both the righteous and the unrighteous. The trials come to us all as well, and each one is appointed to die – and after that, to face judgment. How can we know the day of our death? Indeed, Job, in his troubles, asks why it was that he should even be born. He reasoned in his suffering that it would have been better never to have been born than to see the trouble he now confronts. But our citizenship is in heaven, and we eagerly await a Savior from there, the Lord Jesus Christ.

One day, I will pass on and go to the other side, though I know not the day nor the hour. Then I look forward to that city, whose builder and maker is God. Confident in this, the eye has not seen, nor has any ear heard, nor has it entered into man's mind what God has prepared for those who love him.

I will give him a white stone and on the stone a new name written, which no one knows but he who receives it. Revelation 2:17 NIV

Book 3

In Deep Water

54

DEDICATION

For John and Joey and Janey, each one precious

1 LET IT BE KNOWN

You make known to me the path of life; you will fill me with joy in your presence

Psalm 16:11 NIV

"I'm home!" he called out, coming in through the garage door. It has been a long day. It was clear that some visitors were here.

She greeted him at the door.

"You can see Kaye and Clarise are here. And Essie just called; she and Leon are on the way."

He dropped his backpack laden with books on the floor.

"Really? It's already after 9 pm!" he replied as he went to the fridge to fill a glass of water.

The doorbell rang just then, and Kaye opened the door for the happy couple. They were both holding onto a big bouquet of balloons.

"Guess what, Mommy and Daddy!" Essie said with a beaming smile. Dad had put down his glass of water and joined his wife in the living room to greet the new visitors. The parents now began to suspect the nature of this news.

"Grandchild number four!"

A balloon is an excellent symbol of happiness -beautiful, fun, temporary, and in the end — deflated.

2 REGARDING JOB'S COMPLAINT

*Or why was I not hidden away in the ground like a stillborn child,
like an infant who never saw the light of day?   Job 3:16*

"The doctor said you are going to stay the night. He wants to keep you for observation." It was not a question.

He's concerned about me now, not the baby. The baby is gone.

One tear came into her eye. She did not want to spend the night here. She did not want to lose the child she and Leon had announced with such joy.

"Do you think he's gone?" she turned to Leon. He was silent for a moment.

"We need to take care of you now, babe." That was her answer. The baby was gone, and they both knew it.

"But I'm going to be cold here! My feet always get cold, and we didn't have a chance to prepare!"

"Here you go," Dad said, holding out a pair of socks to Leon, "help her get these on."

"Daddy, what did you do?" Essie asked incredulously.

"I took off my socks. You need them – you can just keep them in fact," he smiled as he spoke. She could see he and Mom were hurt too.

"We will pray for you both, won't we, Mom?"

"Of course. In fact, let's pray now," she replied.

"Thank you, Daddy and Mommy." Tears in her eyes.

He measured off another thousand, but now it was a river that I could not cross, because the water had risen and was deep enough to swim in—a river that no one could cross.
Ezekiel 47:5 NIV

3 DESIRES OF THE HEART

Take delight in the Lord, and he will give you the desires of your heart.

Psalm 37:4 NIV

What do you want?

I want a husband who loves me.

What do you want?

I want a child of my own

Do you want to be safe?

I want the freedom to do hard things.

What are you holding on to?

I can't let them fade away.

You provide a broad path for my feet,
so that my ankles do not give way.   2 Samuel 22:37 (NIV)

4 THE SECOND ANNOUNCEMENT

Elijah climbed to the top of Carmel, bent down to the ground, and put his face between his knees. "Go and look toward the sea," he told his servant. And he went up and looked. "There is nothing there," he said. Seven times Elijah said, "Go back."

1 Kings 18:42 NIV

"Well, it's a yes!" Essie said with a smile.

"Now comes the hard part," Leon replied, "when do we announce this one?"

"Maybe just family this time?" she said as they embraced.

"Yeah, let's play it a slower this time," he whispered as he held her.

"I pray this one is okay," she responded, closing her eyes.

"I hope so too." They separated.

"So, you call your folks, and I call mine?"

She nodded wistfully. "I really wish we could just tell everyone. Shouldn't it be a time of joy?"

We picture something called 'chance' as our sardonic nemesis.

Grant me justice against my adversary.

5 OUT OF TOWN

But tell a stranger, long in tempests toss'd,
What earth we tread, and who commands the coast?
Aeneid Book 1, 437-438

She glanced at the small glass full of water – specially ordered with ice. The sweat drops ran down the stem and gradually stained the white tablecloth. As she picked at her food without looking up, he noticed she was quiet.

"What's wrong, babe?" he asked. She sighed.

"I sort of wish we hadn't told anyone yet," she replied, still not looking up.

"Why not? Do you feel okay?" he spoke with concern. Finally, she looked up at her husband and shrugged.

"I don't know. Feels like maybe something is wrong. A little spotting. Maybe it is nothing," she said with a hopeful smile. He nodded.

"I hope so. We should enjoy this trip."

She picked up the glass and took a sip. She set it down unevenly, and the water spilled out across the small table.

She started to cry.

"I am a foreigner and stranger among you. Sell me some property for a burial site here so I can bury my dead." Genesis 23:4 NIV

6 IN THE NAME

*Now the LORD God had formed out of the ground all the wild animals and all the birds
in the sky. He brought them to the man to see what he would name them; and whatever
the man called each living creature, that was its name. Genesis 2:19 NIV*

Why did you give them names?

Because they were real.

Why do the names all start with the letter 'J'?

So they would have something in common.

What words did you not want to learn?

Spontaneous abortion, recurrent miscarriage

What is the smallest act of kindness?

A finger dipped in cool water then touched to the tongue of the one in torment

What is the next smallest act of kindness?

To receive a covering when you are cold.

*If he snatches away, who can stop him?
Who can say to him, 'What are you doing?' Job 9:12 (NIV)*

7 TAKING MY LEAVE

What grieved them most was his statement that they would never see his face again. Then they accompanied him to the ship.

Acts 20:38 (NIV)

She was there

And now I'm gone

I never said goodbye.

Can't see her tears

Can't calm my fears

Didn't want her to die

She told me

   tears in her eyes

She told me

   to come Home

She was there

But now I'm gone

We never said goodbye.

I have let you see it with your eyes, but you will not cross over into it.

Deuteronomy 34:4

8 A TIME TO PRAY

Lord, teach us to pray

Luke 11:1 NIV

Dear Father in Heaven,

Holy is your name! Thank you for your steadfast love, your grace, and your mercies, which are new every morning. In everything, I give you thanks. In all circumstances, even in the deepest of waters, I will rejoice knowing that your steadfast love and faithfulness are beyond measure.

Grant me now a child according to your will and your great purpose. May the child be devoted to you and grow in knowledge and stature, and in favor with God and people. May the child be a source of joy to us and result in overflowing thanksgiving and glory to you, O Father.

Humbly I ask, knowing that in your great power, you can accomplish more than I can even ask or imagine.

In Jesus' name,

Amen.

…but God has surely listened and has heard my prayer.

Psalms 66:1 NIV

9 A WINTER SUN

when the waters become hard as stone

when the surface of the deep is frozen? Job 38:30 NIV

"I can do this," she announced as he pulled the car into the cemetery.

"Yeah, but you know you don't have to. After what we have been through. I mean, everyone would understand," he replied while looking for a place to park.

"I told Kaye I would do it. It's hard, which is exactly why I want to do it," she said firmly.

There were over fifty people there already. Only about twelve chairs were available under the tent for the family. She looked up at the winter sky as they made their way towards the tent. The sun seemed distant and cold.

It was her turn to speak.

It says in Psalms 94 that the Lord knows all of our plans. And it says he knows they are futile… We don't plan tragedies like this… But Jeremiah reminds us that God has plans for us…. Plans to give us hope and a future… In Psalms 100, David tells us that the Lord is good, and his love endures forever. We can be confident in his love and goodness.

She glanced at her parents on the front row. She could see their sorrow mixed with pride.

He speaks to the sun, and it does not shine; he seals off the light of the stars.

Job 9:7 NIV

10 FOYER OF SOULS

The angel measured the wall using human measurement

Revelation 21:17 (NIV)

An angel stands with an open scroll.

"Janey – for this is the name which your mother and father will use – you are now being sent."

"To what purpose?" asked the soul-being.

"You are sent but to dip your finger into the river of time," the angel replied, still examining the scroll.

"But how will I find my way back here?" the soul-being replied.

"Fear not – my fellow worker will be there to guide you back to this place," the angel said, now looking up at the soul-being.

"How will I know him?" asked the soul-being.

"You need not know him. He knows you. Even if I told you his appearance, it would be in vain, for you will not remember this conversation. Go now, for you are sent."

He makes his angels spirits, and his servants flames of fire

Hebrews 1:7 (NIV)

11 HIDDEN SORROW

Then birds of prey came down on the carcasses, but Abram drove them away.

As the sun was setting, Abram fell into a deep sleep, and a thick and dreadful darkness came over him.

Genesis 15:11,12 NIV

They both had tears and found it difficult to speak. When the doctor told them the numbers, they didn't need to ask what it meant. They shuffled quietly out of the office and began walking back to the car.

"I'm glad we didn't tell anyone. Except Kaye and Levi, of course," he began.

"I don't even want to tell anyone we lost a third one. Our parents have been through enough with the loss of Violet. They don't need to hear about this," she said in anguish.

"Maybe we should still tell them. You know they would want to know," he suggested.

"Do you think we will ever have a baby?" she asked, desperately hoping he would say 'yes.'

Come to me, all you who are weary and burdened, and I will give you rest.

Matthew 11:28 NIV

12 THOUGHTS ON THE SANDPIPER

… you fill me with joy in your presence Psalm 16:11 (NIV)

Have you seen the sandpiper, which I created? Her feathers are dull and drab. She digs her daily food out of the mud and sand with her long legs and narrow bill. Will you not wonder at her form and take joy in seeing this tiny bird fulfill her purpose, the purpose for which I created her?

When you see her on the sand, will you not look up and say, "See, the joy! She is drab, even ungainly, yet she carries out her daily work!"

So too, when the drabness of grief and loss overshadow you, take joy in the daily bread, which I have provided for you. When you see the sandpiper on the beach, let it bring you joy. Then go and fulfill the purpose for which I created you.

All my longings lie open before you, Lord; my sighing is not hidden from you.
Psalm 38:9 (NIV)

13 A TIME TO HEAL

a time to kill and a time to heal, a time to tear down and a time to build

Ecclesiastes 3:3 NIV

There is a time to heal, but it is not time that heals. A person who has bled to death does not get better with time. Putting blood back into the dead body will not help either – the body is dead!

Where there is life, there can be healing. The process of healing takes time, but it is the healing that heals, not time. Our bodies were designed by God to be self-healing. When we get cut, signals go throughout the body to begin the process- stopping the bleeding, fighting off infection, and restoring the wounded flesh. We can help the healing from the outside by cleaning the wound, covering it, and favoring it to keep it from further injury.

Healing is good; therefore, God is the ultimate cause of healing. The process will take time. Does a farmer plant seeds and look for crops the next day? No, the farmer waits patiently for the rain and the sunshine to do their work. In due time, the harvest will come.

So too, ask for healing from the Healer. Then wait patiently and believe.

Do I have the strength of stone? Is my flesh bronze?

Job 6:12 NIV

14 OVERCOMING

A woman giving birth to a child has pain because her time has come; but when her baby is born, she forgets the anguish because of her joy that a child is born into the world.

John 16:21 NIV

"Is everything packed?" he asked, ready to zip up the hospital 'go' bag.

"One more thing!" she called out from the bedroom as she rummaged through the dresser. Then she went out into the living room, holding the missing item. He was confused at first but then recognized them.

"THOSE socks. I thought you just wanted one more pair of socks," he said, laughing a little.

"You remember these then?"

"Yes, I have seen you wear them sometimes. But don't they bring back bad memories?"

"Sometimes, yes. It is all hard to look back on. They also remind me of Daddy's love, which then reminds me of God's love. Yeah, I'm going to wear them when Aaron is born." He took the socks from her hand and put them into the bag.

"Let's do this then," he said, slinging the bag over his shoulder and taking his wife's hand.

Build up, build up, prepare the road! Remove the obstacles out of the way of my people.

Isaiah 57:14 NIV

15 ARRIVAL

Do I bring to the moment of birth and not give delivery?" says the Lord.
Isaiah 66:9 NIV

"He's here! Can you believe it?" she spoke softly, holding the tiny newborn in her arms.

"Yup! There he is!" Leon was as close as he could be, touching the little hand and watching his son curl his hand around the finger.

"We prayed for you! We've been waiting for you! Finally, here you are," she spoke tenderly to her son. She looked up at Leon.

"Get your phone! We must capture this moment. Make sure you get me and Aaron AND the socks in the picture."

I waited patiently for the Lord; he inclined and heard my cry. He brought me up out of the pit, out of the miry clay. I will sing a new song!

From Psalm 40 KJV, paraphrase by author

16 SONG OF JOY

Sing, barren woman, you who never bore a child
Isaiah 54:1 NIV

Sing for now you can present the child to your family

You can place the babe in your mother's arms

And see your father smile with pride.

Sing for the joy of motherhood and fatherhood

Rejoice that you can see your child with your own eyes

And hold him in your arms.

Sing that God bore you up in the deep waters

Rejoice that your faith was tested and found strong

And that you did not shrink or faint in the trial.

17 A MOM'S DEDICATION DISCOURSE

Today is a special day. It's one I've thought about long before we even knew Aaron was on his way because I knew when we got here, it would be a testimony of Gods love and faithfulness. What was the purpose of this heartache? What was the plan? Were we not meant to be parents? We waited, and we prayed. Nearly a year later, amidst an extremely difficult season for my family and me, we lost our third baby. I despaired. We'd lost my grandmother, my precious niece Violet, and now this baby in a very short period. I was angry and felt hopeless and beaten down.

It's okay to have questions if we take them to God. The Bible is full of promises. I think these promises are meant to sustain us in hard times. They give hope to the hopeless. I don't know why our story went this way, but I know it made me realize that life isn't always easy, but God promised us we'd never be alone. A verse I read over and over during this time Is from Isiah 43; God is speaking to the Israelites, and He says, *2 When you go through deep waters,   I will be with you. When you go through rivers of difficulty,   you will not drown. When you walk through the fire of oppression,   you will not be burned up;   the flames will not consume you. 3 For I am the Lord, your God,   the Holy One of Israel, your Savior.*

As I cried out to God in the days following this third heartache, I felt him speak a promise over our life. We would have a child. I felt hope again. I also felt strongly that God was saying it would be a while before we had this child. This promise sustained us during the following months. The next fall, nearly a year and a half after our third loss, we found out we were pregnant for a fourth time.

If you are hurting today, if you feel hopeless or broken-hearted from waiting, I pray you seek hope and healing in Gods word and his promises

EPILOGUE - I SAY TO YOU

A little girl lies dying. The mother will stay with the child while the father goes to seek help. But where will he go?

"I will go to the Healer," he tells his wife, "for there is no one else to whom we can turn."

With quick and anxious steps, he seeks him out. There he is! The father makes his way through the crowd and falls at his feet.

"Please come! My little girl is dying! Please come and touch her so that she will be healed!"

So, the Healer came with him. On the way, the dreaded news comes. The mother has sent word that the child has died. Why bother the healer now? The report is whispered to the father, but the Healers hears and knows. Indeed, he sees the news in the father's expression.

He speaks two commands: Fear not. Believe.

The crowd of mourners surround the house. The Healer sends them away and brings only his closest friends and the father and mother to the room. There lies the young girl. The crowd says she is dead. The senses and reason agree she is dead.

But the Healer says she is asleep. He gently lifts her little hand and takes it in his. Then he speaks to her.

"Little girl, I say to you, get up!"

Do not be discouraged for your little ones who have fallen asleep.

O do not be uninformed about those who sleep in death!

The Healer can wake them up at any moment in his divine will. If it is not now, at the father and the mother's urgent request, the day will come. One day, it will be that Day.

Then he will come with trumpet sound, and with a loud command to all who sleep, He will call out:

"I say to you, get up!"

And all those who have fallen asleep in Him will arise to be with Him forever. So shall we all who believe be united with Him.

Forever.

Fear not.

Believe.